Poems

String of thoughts

Gulshan Kumar

BookLeaf Publishing
India | USA | UK

Made with ❤ on the BookLeaf Publishing Platform
www.bookleafpub.in
www.bookleafpub.com

Dedication

I dedicate this book to lost friends.

Preface

In the quiet moments of our lives, when the world slows down and the noise fades away, poetry finds its voice. It is in these moments that we turn to the written word to capture the essence of our emotions, the beauty of our surroundings, and the complexity of our thoughts. This collection of poems is a journey through such moments, an exploration of the human experience in its myriad forms.

Poetry has the unique ability to distill the vastness of life into a few carefully chosen words, to paint vivid pictures with the simplest of phrases. It speaks to the heart, bypassing the barriers of language and culture, and resonates with the universal truths that bind us all. In this book, you will find poems that reflect on love and loss, joy and sorrow, hope and despair. Each piece is a reflection of the world as seen through the eyes of the poet, offering a glimpse into the soul and inviting the reader to pause and reflect.

The poems in this collection are not just words on a page; they are an invitation to engage with the world in a deeper, more meaningful way. They challenge us to see beyond the surface, to find beauty in the mundane, and to appreciate the fleeting nature of life. Whether you are a seasoned reader of poetry or new to the genre, I hope that these poems will speak to you, offering solace, inspiration, and a sense of connection.

As you turn the pages of this book, may you find moments of reflection and revelation. May the words within these pages stir your imagination and touch your heart. And may you discover, as I have, the enduring power of poetry to illuminate the human spirit.

Welcome to this journey of words and emotions. May it be as enriching for you as it has been for me.

Acknowledgements

I would like to extend my deepest gratitude to everyone who has supported me throughout this journey. To my family, who never understood poetry but never intervened to stop me. To my friends, whose patience, insight, and belief in me kept me going during the toughest of times. Special thanks to all the 4 instagram readers.

1. Can you forgive me?

Can you ever forgive me,
For all the times I wasn't there,
For the times I didn't care?

Can you ever forgive me,
For all the pain that we shared,
For all the times I was a nightmare?

Can you ever forgive me,
For all the sad letters I wrote,
And for all the annoying notes?

Can you ever forgive me,
For all my expectations,
For all my impatient passions?

2. Maybe I want to die

Can you ever forgive me,
For all the times I wasn't there,
For the times I didn't care?

Can you ever forgive me,
For all the pain that we shared,
For all the times I was a nightmare?

Can you ever forgive me,
For all the sad letters I wrote,
And for all the annoying notes?

Can you ever forgive me,
For all my expectations,
For all my impatient passions?

3. Fault in our stars

There are those dark, silent nights
Where I wish you were with me in those hours of eternal
sorrow,
Holding me through the darkness,
And we could just talk about something 'til morrow.

I know you can't;
You are different,
And we aren't supposed to be together.
And I know, if you knew what I meant, you would be
seen nowhere.

I wonder why I always get enchanted by forbidden fruit,
Like you, my dear.
I talk to you while always composing myself,
Keeping my heart's little secret away so you don't have
anything to fear.

The double ways of my life:
One when I am alone, fantasizing about you and leaving
myself with innumerable scars,
And the other with you, trying to be just someone you
know.

The fault, dear love, is not in us; maybe it's just in our stars.

4. The Weight of Stillness

The nights are without moon or a single star,
It's dark, and I lie down on the roof,
Wondering at the vastness of nothingness,
And thinking if it is just an extension of my own soul.
I wish it would change,
The mundane morning routines,
The evening talks which constitute boredom and pain,
Living the same day over and over again.
I want this darkness to wrap me,
And I can let go of hope,
Of dreams and desires,
Of so many lingering fires.
I just want to lie here,
'Til the end of everything,
And I'll let go of my breath with gentleness,
As if nothing has changed; yet everything will change.

5. Of Trees and Seasons

A tree in my backyard is old and dying,
It was there when I came here,
Even then, it was old and dying,
And I wonder if it was always old and dying.

It has witnessed the spring of joy,
When children sometimes climbed,
Sometimes played around with their changing toys,
And then, one day, those children were replaced by teens
who were coy.

It has witnessed the summer of temptations,
Of innocent attempts to feel love,
And their flood of emotions,
Of recitals of poems of adoration and accusations.

It has witnessed the autumn of old age,
Losing hair and sometimes the joy of life,
And then slowly descending into the winter of death,
with no fight, no rage,
And then they are gone, while the tree lives on, old and
dying.

6. Kabul has fallen

Light some fire in the sky,
It's getting too dark,
All roads lead to nowhere,
Maybe I am scared.

Kabul has fallen,
Children are dead,
Lots have been said; nothing is now done,
Please do something.

All eyes are now behind a veil,
All the dreams are now lost,
In the smoke of bullets,
And under the trample of boots.

No promises are broken,
As none were made,
The trees of freedom are burned,
And we watch with horror and stupor.

7. Never wrote a good poetry

I never wrote a single good poem,
My diaries are filled with the gibberish of a broken man,
Of unstructured lines filled with grief and pain,
As if the ink has been washed away in bizarre rain.

I never recited anything meaningful,
Maybe I never found any meaning.
My words carried no notes of music,
And my ears and soul had damaged acoustics.

My stories were always unfinished,
With plots teetering while awaiting the perfect
conclusion,
And characters sorrowful, vengeful, and in perfect
collusion.
I am an unreasonable man, trying to reason.

My letters were never posted,
Kept between journals of bad poetry and incomplete
prose,
Hidden only partially between pages like a scandalous
affair,
Awaiting their fate, alike their owner.

8. There will be blood

I am the sinner,
And the play is over,
Now I will crawl through the mud,
And there will be blood.

I am left with no prayer,
All I have is a longing stare,
There will be sprinkles on the new bud,
And yes, there will be blood.

Ah! A new man is weaving a new tale,
Hoping to tame the winds of destiny with his youthful
sail,
Oblivious to the tune of the impending flood,
And yes, just like in every good tale, there will be blood.

Men's lust is wrapped in pious exchange of promises,
Sins are wrapped in youthful kisses,
And when these fragile wrappers are torn apart in
adulthood,
There will be tears, and there will be blood.

9. One day

One day,
I will tell everyone
Every beautiful thing about them,
And capture their smile on my camera.

One day,
I will tell that one person
How much I liked her all these years,
And how her response doesn't matter now.

One day,
I will tell that one person
Every fantasy of mine,
And my helpless smile will mirror hers.

One day,
I will roam the city as a vagabond,
Without thinking of time,
As there would be nothing to care about.

10. Who do you care for?

Did you pull the curtains
Before you cried alone in the room?
Did you let go of all hope
Before you kissed the darkness and gloom?

If everything is gone,
What do you wait for?
If you are so alone,
Whom do you care for?

11. The Facade of Ordinary

The boring man will go to the office in plain attire,
Hiding his own colorful desire,
Desire that is dark and dangerous,
And dreams that are too scandalous.
He will look at you as if he is curious,
Giving a half smile, painful or just mysterious.
Looking at the screen throughout the day,
Sometimes just stealing a gaze out of the window bay,
As if smiling and reminiscing about gone days,
Which are truly gone,
And a lullaby of music is sung, leaving him alone.
Nothing to cheer or to moan,
All moments seem the same,
Or the same moment just repeating, like a slow song on
a fast loop.
He will greet you,
When he meets you,
Will have nothing left to say.
The boring man will find you boring.
He will head home listening to some wild songs,
Songs of thug life, cheating wife, bloodlust knife,
Songs of upbeat despair and cynic inspiration,
Songs of war and love, all in the name of the nation.
Folk songs too, with melody,

And rap songs by Slim Shady.
In an hour trip, he goes through everything—
Memories, emotions, and thoughts flashing.
Memories of the last loved one,
Feeling special pity for himself, like anyone and
everyone.
Pity for the flower-selling girl,
Whose smile is like a dark but shiny pearl.
Hating capitalism,
Wearing Adidas, listening to iTunes.
Hypocrites are too immune.
Drowns in the cold shower,
Washing down his sins for an hour.
Standing naked with an ugly paunch in front of the
mirror,
Trying to force a smile—
A smile which is ugly and vile.
His smile has now caught up with his fury,
He is the convict, prosecutor, judge, and jury.
He is going to watch Netflix and chill,
Have a fancy meal,
While thinking about swallowing those blissful pills.
He will leave hell for heaven,
Heaven, where he wins and she loses,
Where he is both god and messenger, like Moses,
Where his smile is beautiful and perfect,
No paunch, looking like Brad or Benedict.

All fair and muscular,
Cool like a true hustler.
Until the cruel voice of the morning bird invades his
paradise,
And paradise is lost.
All that's left is plain attire to dress,
To eat is half-burnt toast,
Room looking like a mess.
A day too long and dark,
Like the fate of every Stark.
Soul to be executed with no trial,
Fake smile,
Wrong number to dial,
Anger hidden,
Lover forgotten,
Love forbidden.
Feeling the taste of the capitalist world,
Ecstatic but hollow, just like the aftermath of
masturbation.
The boring man in his plain attire
Lives another day.
That's the way,
The only way.

12. The small Giraffe

I once met a small giraffe,
The giraffe was adult, not a calf,
Yet she was not tall,
So I made a call.
A call to the zoo,
After listening to the predicament, they made a boo.
So I took the giraffe to a jungle,
And other giraffes laughed and made a rumble.
The small giraffe felt sad and humbled,
Took a deep breath and mumbled.

She now lives in the city,
And feels superior among others' mediocrity.
Her temper flares as others are small,
Yet she too trips and falls.

13. If I die today

If I die today,
And tomorrow you find my lifeless body,
Let it lie,
Don't try to revive.

In the drawer of my untidy desk will be my unposted
letters,
Burn them,
Burn them along with my diaries,
Diaries that contain my hazy thoughts,
Thoughts incomplete, broken, and of brief grief.

Don't go through my purse, which has a photo of a lost
lover,
Lost irretrievably in time,
Time which swallowed me slowly.

Burn my clothes, books, and all signs of me,
And my perverse existence,
And my coward-filled reluctance.

Don't let sorrow come upon you,
For there's nothing to mourn,
No one to remember.

14. For Turing

One day, they came and took him away,
They told him that he had done something wrong,
Asked him to be calm and strong,
Without letting him know what exactly was at play.

They say he was a soldier,
Or an inventor, or some field's pioneer,
A legend, a man—
His crime was him being sane.

The charges, as they were read,
And then everyone said,
He isn't the man built from the same mold,
No one he had hurt, but his choices were peculiar and
too bold.

Prison and probation,
Followed by some chemical experimentation,
He was let free,
But void of any freedom.

The tragedy of injustice,
Witnessed by everyone, but all were Nero's guests.
Today we have plaques and awards in his memory,

Hopefully now buried, his unfilled life has some peace and rest.

15. I don't like you

I don't like you,
You, who use correct words,
And polished language.
Alas, my thoughts are rugged and fragmented,
A reflection of my soul.

I don't like you,
You, who are 'subtle' and 'diplomatic,'
Covering your hypocrisy beneath these refined words,
Who have lost all capability for honesty.

I don't like you,
You, who crawl when asked to bend,
Kissing the devil and making mends,
Caring more for feelings than facts,
More for perception than events.

I don't like you,
You, who exist to survive,
Stand by and watch people burn,
Silent, convenient, and blind with both eyes open,
Like Nero's guests.

16. Matrimonial

Wanted,
A girl who is fair,
Just enough, because my complexion is inferior.
English-educated, but should learn not to aspire.

I am standing with my token,
A token of penis, caste, and religion.
And girl, your hymen mustn't be broken.
If I read other ads, then only my conscience will be
woken.

Don't be Muslim,
It's fine if you have curves, but should be slim.
Your eyes should be beautiful, but void of any dream,
And get rid of that mole with some cream.

My family is a family of culture,
And cultured should you be.
We will swoop low for dowry, as does the great vulture,
And be the Dasi that you dutifully must be.

17. Misery

I don't have a home,
I don't have anywhere to turn to,
No place where I belong,
No people to get along.

I have had a roof everywhere,
And I have had doors closed from inside or/and outside,
But I have always chosen unheard notes of absurd songs,
And everything went wrong that could go wrong.

I have wandered here and there,
With eyes closed and blank stares,
Staying nowhere for too long,
Life's been a long mundane journey with no sight of a
swan song.

There is a path I should take to home,
But I see it every day and let it be,
Seeing it as a frightening unknown.
Maybe the path will exist even after I am gone.

18. Two strangers

In the end,
We are just two strangers,
Wrapped up together in our shared trauma.
We don't speak,
We can't speak.
Words are too weightless to carry our pain,
All our anguish, all our rage, in vain.
We must listen to each other,
Though no one will speak,
No one can speak.
In this desert of loneliness,
We are two strangers held together by our shared
trauma.

19. Lives

I live so many lives,
Yet I exist only in one of them.
I dream so many nightmares,
Yet only my truth haunts me.

My lies, hidden and well taken care of,
Scar my little scared heart,
And give me restless nights,
And gloomy days.

All I want is to be me,
Yet I can't be.
I take refuge in a stranger's kindness,
And then I take flight from a stranger who is now a
companion.

I am tired of running away,
Hiding behind screens of illusion,
Living with my delusions,
With memories of events, which might or might not
have happened.

20. Dark Circles

The dark circles around my eyes tell a story,
A story of sleepless nights,
Blinding lights,
And guilt-ridden dreams.

The dark circles are a testimony
Of when I cried silently all through the night,
When she was gone,
And of desperate nights when no one picked up my
phone.

The dark circles are memories of those desolate nights,
When I grieved my dead friends,
Over and over again,
And yet couldn't let go of the blinding pain.

The dark circles are growing darker,
As I live once and die a thousand times a night,
Trying to evade the noose of my own shadow,
Knowing well that I have long ago given up the fight.

21. To all whom I loved

I wish you were never gone,
All of you who were here,
At some moment or other,
Now your name remains as part of my heart's murmur.
Under the starlit sky,
We made promises which we couldn't keep,
Our feelings, so much on the surface,
Yet the wounds are so deep.
Our memories will fade,
And so will our pain,
Hopefully, like me, you don't have any regret,
Or any "if"—was it all for nothing, in vain?
There are burning pyres on the river,
And as I write these last lines in your memories,
In the morning of a cold November,
I remember you all with some warmth.